What  are Saying...

"*The Seven Characters of Abuse* is a must read for anyone who wants to have an increased understanding and insight into abusive relationships and how to avoid them. The authors use both their personal and professional experience to point out the often subtle, yet emotionally lethal dynamics behind these very dangerous personalities. They also empower their readers to look for and know the danger signs before it's too late."

—**Dr. Robi Ludwig,** *Psychotherapist and Author of Till Death Do Us Part: Love, Marriage, and the Mind of the Killer Spouse*

"Tanya and Carolyn have written a very important book in which they give hope to thousands of women who may not be feeling hopeful. If I could make a wish for these women, I would wish that they would read this book and find hope for the future and courage to make decisions for their own happiness."

—**Frank Shankwitz,** *Founder/Creator of Make A Wish Foundation www.Wishman1.com*

"Both Tanya and Carolyn have transformed *The Seven Characters of Abuse* into a powerful teaching tool!"

—**Laura Cowan,** *Founder of*
The Laura Cowan Foundation for Battered Women
www.TheLauraCowanStory.net
https://m.facebook.com/TheLauraCowanFoundation

"It's amazing to think that my father embodied all seven characters — sometimes individually and, at times, collectively. I strongly recommend this book! It will be a great resource in many settings, including academically."

—**Victor Rivers,** *Actor, Athlete, Activist and Author of*
the bestselling memoir, A Private Family Matter
www.VictorRivers.com

"In this important little book, Tanya and Carolyn have provided the opportunity for women to identify with other women who are in hurtful relationships. It will be hard for them to stay in denial after reading the examples of real women who were being controlled by the men in their lives. And, it doesn't end there. There is help, hope, and resources for action."

—**Erik Swanson,** *Author of*
The Habitude Warrior: 50 Secret Habitudes
www.HabitudeWarrior.com

"As a former Olympian, I have had the privilege of relating with individuals from all over the world. There are some things that unite all people no matter where they are from, and one of them is power. This book will help women become able to recognize the difference between a healthy love and unhealthy power and control."

—**Ruben Gonzalez,** *FOUR-time Luge Olympian and Author of*
The Courage to Succeed: Success Secrets of
an Unlikely Four-time Olympian
www.Ruben-Gonzalez.com

"With the World Health Organization reporting that 1 in 3 American women will experience physical or sexual violence by an intimate partner, Tanya and Carolyn's new book offers important warning signs and exit strategies for those who find themselves in potentially dangerous relationships. I am hopeful that the book will spark a much-needed dialogue around this national epidemic."

—**Lori Vandermeir,** *Head of Communications, United States*
National Committee for United Nations Women
Former President, National Organization for Women
(Orange County, California)
www.StrategicCommunicationConsultants.com

"This is an important book on an important topic that will serve many. Read this book, then pass it along to help others!"

—**James Malinchak,** *Featured on ABCs Hit*
TV Show, "Secret Millionaire"
Top-Selling Author of Millionaire Success Secrets
Founder of www.MillionaireFreeBook.com

"Tanya and Carolyn have made the process of identifying the signs of abuse easy to understand and, more importantly, a quick read for those who may suspect that they or a dear friend or loved one are being abused. When time is of the essence, a 'pocket guide' is essential. They have made it easy for friends, family members, and co-workers to identify the behavior and talk to their friend about a very difficult subject. Thank you, Tanya and Carolyn, for breaking this down for us."

—**Sherri Loveland,** *President of*
National Women's Political Caucus of California
www.NWPCCA.org

"Tanya and Carolyn share wisdom and tools for those wanting to get out, become aware, or heal from abuse. They share extensive information and education to help the reader to be empowered and strong, and to rise above hardships into a life of triumph and greatness. I highly recommend this book to anyone wanting awareness and knowledge. It is life-changing in a huge way."

—**Kim Somers Egelsee,** *Confidence Expert and*
Author of Get Your Life to a 10+
www.KimLifeCoach.com

The Seven Characters of Abuse

Domestic Violence: Where It Starts and Where It Can End

Tanya Brown and Carolyn Inmon

The Seven Characters of Abuse
Domestic Violence:
Where It Starts and Where It Can End

by
Tanya Brown, M.A. in Counseling Psychology
Carolyn Inmon, M.A. in Speech Communication

Published by
Abundant Press
www.AbundantPress.com

www.7CharactersOfAbuseBook.com
www.TanyaBrown.net
www.CarolynInmonStopDomesticAbuse.com

Disclaimer: The Publisher and the Author do not guarantee that anyone following the techniques, suggestions, tips, ideas or strategies will become successful. The advice and strategies contained herein may not be suitable for every situation. The Publisher and Author shall have neither liability nor responsibility to anyone with respect to any loss or damage caused, or alleged to be caused, directly or indirectly by the information in this book. Any citations or a potential source of information from other organizations or websites given herein does not mean that the Author or Publisher endorses the information/content the website or organization provides or recommendations it may make. It is the readers' responsibility to do their own due diligence when researching information. Also, websites listed or referenced herein may have changed or disappeared from the time that this work was created and the time that it is read.

Disclaimer: *We, Tanya Brown and Carolyn Inmon, are not licensed physicians, therapists, or mental health practitioners. Life Coaches, Speakers, and Educators do not diagnose conditions, nor do they prescribe or perform medical treatment, prescribe substances, nor interfere with the treatment of a licensed medical professional. Do understand that coaching, teachings and information in this book do not take the place of medical or psychological care.*

It is recommended that you see a licensed physician or licensed mental health care professional for any physical or psychological issues you may have.

ISBN:

Printed in the United States of America

Dedication

To Tanya's sister, Nicole, for giving us the voice to save so many who are victims and survivors of domestic violence. Silence no more. In your name, we speak out to save lives.

To Tanya's dad, Lou Brown, for founding the Nicole Brown Foundation. The organization, now closed, provided urgently-needed funding to battered women shelters across the country. The Brown family immersed themselves in the education of the cycle of violence.

To Human Options, for being the shelter who first educated us on domestic violence. Without them, we would not understand the issue nearly as well as we do.

Lastly, to the women and children inflicted with abuse, may you stay strong and courageous!

Thank You

Thank you to everyone for believing in this message and supporting this important outreach.

Thank you to our team leaders, especially:

Amanda Johnson, CEO of True to Intention and our writing coach, who helped us evolve as authors and gave her kind and capable support to our work.

Andy Broadaway, of Innovative Digital Marketing Strategies, our marketing expert, whose brilliant strategies are helping us to reach more women.

Steve Huang, MBA | 黃仕文, Principal Business Consultant, CSC DG, Carolyn's Facebook and website creator whose wisdom, expertise, and patience helped move ideas into beautiful social network works of art.

Dan Mulhern and Michael Hooper, Tanya's XCEL Creative team, whose patience, compassion, inspiration, and incredible support has helped us get our message out into the world. Along with Krystal Reyes, this team opened up the world of social media to us.

Thank you to Casey Gwinn, whose response to our message in his Foreword is so understanding, positive, and insightful.

Thank you to our <u>endorsers</u> for taking the time to read our book and craft such beautiful endorsements.

Thank you to <u>John</u>, Carolyn's husband, a good man who makes it easy to have a healthy relationship. Thank you for your nurturing and consistent support.

Thank you to everyone who shares our passion to help women and whose support allows us to reach more and more women every day. Thank you so much for everything!

Huge Hugs!

Tanya Brown
Carolyn Inmon

Contents

Foreword

By Casey Gwinn, Esq.

Too often when we talk about domestic violence, we focus only on physical and sexual abuse. But the foundation of violent and abusive relationships is usually, at its core, based on emotionally abusive behaviors. Some relationships then evolve into physical and sexual violence. Other relationships never become physically violent, but one partner endures a relationship filled with emotional, spiritual, and verbal abuse.

Tanya Brown and Carolyn Inmon have done a great job of providing a short, straightforward, practical book for better understanding manipulative and controlling men — characters, as they call them. From the "Jealous Stalker" to the "Silent Knight", they provide profiles of emotionally abusive men that victimize millions of women day in and day out across the United States and around the world.

This short book can help many impacted by power and control behaviors in an intimate relationship, even where there may be no physical or sexual violence yet or ever. Evaluate your own relationship as you read this book or give it to a friend that may be stuck in an unhealthy dating relationship or marriage.

As a child, I remember watching crabs sitting in water on the San Francisco waterfront, that were to become a delightful cuisine. The chefs never put the crabs in hot water. They always put the crabs in cold water and then heated it up to a boil. By the time the water was deadly, it was too late for the crabs to jump out. This book is for those in a relationship where the water is warming. Perhaps not yet boiling but getting dangerously hot and they are having trouble realizing just how much heartbreak lies ahead. Those stuck in unhealthy relationships would do well to hold up their relationship and measure it against the stories and examples in this book. It is an easy read and well worth it for anyone who wants to measure their relationship against both the emotionally abusive ones and the healthy relationships offered in each chapter.

Many victims of relationship abuse come to believe it is normal and that all relationships are like their own. Tanya and Carolyn not only give us the ugly side of unhealthy relationships, but they also give us examples of healthy relationships and affirming, uplifting interactions to compare against the ugly controlling behaviors that many begin to settle into.

Tanya knows of what she writes and shares. She lived through the nightmare of the murder of her sister, Nicole Brown Simpson. Then she lived through the impact of the trauma of such unimaginable loss in her own life. Trauma in our own lives as children or adults often leads us into unhealthy coping behaviors and even unhealthy relationships as we fail to process our own pain and loss. So, read on. Even if you are not in an emotionally abusive relationship, this book will better equip you to help family members and friends. We can all be better equipped to spot emotionally abusive partners and the patterns we or those we care about so often get stuck in through the journey of life.

Casey Gwinn, President
Alliance for HOPE International
Author, *Cheering for the Children*

INTRODUCTION
Where It Starts

"You're fat! You're stupid! You're ugly! You cannot do anything right! Where are you going to go? You don't have any skills! You are WORTHLESS!!! You are a fat pig, you are disgusting, you are a fat slob, and I want you out of my %*&$ing house! Let me tell you how serious I am. I have a gun in my hand right now...get the %*&$ out of here."

This is what the famous football player said to Tanya's sister, Nicole.

This is how it started.

You know how it ended — in a courtyard in Brentwood.

"Silence killed my sister," Tanya has said repeatedly.

This book is *not* about physical violence. It is about the lesser understood type of violence: Emotional Abuse. All of the smaller acts of emotional violence that happened before that fateful day in Brentwood — that happen to millions of people on a daily basis.

Emotional abuse is the most hidden kind of domestic abuse. It is not as easily seen and, in fact, can be extremely subtle. It is often confusing, minimized, or ignored, but its effects are real, deep, and long-lasting. Bruises from physical abuse are black and blue while bruises from emotional abuse are hidden and internal.

If the Abuse Isn't Physical, Then What is It?

It is power and control.

- The abuser <u>hits</u> with criticism and verbal put downs.
- He <u>strikes</u> with shame and humiliation.
- He <u>threatens</u> to increase fear and decrease feelings of safety.
- He <u>knocks out</u> self-esteem, self-confidence, and self-respect.
- He <u>smashes</u> serenity and peace of mind.
- He <u>takes away</u> spontaneity, making others walk on eggshells around him.
- He <u>abolishes</u> support systems and leaves the victim lonely and depressed.

His goal is to intimidate, isolate, confuse, and control.

During this beginning phase of domestic violence, tension and stress build up. To some extent, it is suppressed and eventually will explode. During this phase, the abuser may pick fights (not physical acts), act jealous and possessive, criticize, threaten, and be moody or unpredictable.

Through all of our experience and research, we have identified *The Seven Characters of Abuse* that precede physical violence — seven ways this emotional abuse can be expressed.

Each of the Seven Characters can exist independently. For instance, a man can engage in cyber stalking and never hit you, or he could take your money without ever lifting a violent finger in your direction. Whether a man practices one of these seven behaviors as an independent act or engages in several of them as he escalates to physical violence doesn't matter. Each of the seven are behaviors that you do not have to accept.

Because these kinds of abuse often go unacknowledged, it's important to take a good look at them — to become able to identify and recognize these Characters and then decide if you want them in your life. Ultimately, you could be saving your life with this decision. Everything begins somewhere and the Seven Characters are the beginning of the cycle of domestic violence.

Now, it's one thing to have characteristics of abuse explained, but it's quite another to meet a Character that reminds you of the person you are wondering about. Our purpose for filling the book with stories is to make it extremely easy for you to identify whether you are (or someone you love is) actually in an abusive relationship and, toward the end, help you to begin to take careful steps to get (them) out.

We believe it's not only time for our society to admit that emotional abuse exists, is harmful, and affects generations, it's imperative that we all become aware of where it starts and where it can end. It's time to understand it and erase some of the myths and misunderstandings prevalent in our society about what abuse is and who it happens to.

Women that are more likely to become victims are often one of the following: (1) women from families where abuse existed, (2) women who were yelled at and then given excessive love, and (3) women who were disrespected as children.

Yet there are also women who came from very healthy and loving families. Nobody is excluded. Domestic violence neither sees nor hears any boundaries. It does not see race, color, creed, socioeconomic status, or religion. It can happen to anyone who breathes the air on this planet. Many women know they are becoming miserable but don't recognize it as abuse.

Are you one of them?

Our goal with this book is to help people understand this confusing type of abuse and, if they are actually victims, to realize that their relationships are abusive and that it may be time to face the fear, see the signs, uncover the abuse, and discard the abuser. It is possible to end domestic violence, the fear, and the pain by ending the relationship. (We know, easier said than done. But it IS possible. Keep reading.)

We understand that right now you may be feeling anxious, scared, terrified. But we encourage you to keep reading and stay open to the possibility that life could be better and full of real love for you or the loved one you're concerned about.

We've included some questions to support you as you read, hoping that you will take time to reflect on your experiences and especially your feelings in the writing space included next to the questions. Please take the time, no matter how scared you may feel.

It is in the *feeling* that the *healing* can begin.

Let's check in and make sure this is the book for you before we get started!

1. Is your inner voice telling you that something is wrong?

2. Is there something missing in your life: Joy? Spontaneity? Genuine feelings? Positive companionship?

3. Is someone bullying you or humiliating you in front of your children, family or friends?

4. Is the jealousy and anger of your partner making you anxious?

5. Do you find yourself making excuses for your partner?

6. Do you feel that no matter how hard you try you can never do anything right?

7. Do you feel that you aren't smart enough to be in the relationship?

8. Do you sometimes feel you are going crazy?

9. Does it feel that your soul is sad?

10. Do you feel invisible — not just your non-physical wounds but your whole being?

If you answered yes to any of these questions…this book is for you!

NOTE:

By the way, since we believe that privacy is one of the most important aspects of maintaining anonymity and safety, we have protected people by changing the names in the examples.

1

Jealous Stalker

The jealous stalker keeps track of his lady friend, not out of love but out of jealousy and the need to control her. At first, it may look like love, and it's easy for the victim to confuse his control with love. This is NOT love. It is control. The stalker is constantly checking up on her, wanting to know her every move, where she is going, when she is coming back, how long she has been gone, and with whom she is spending her time.

Today, with technology, it's even easier for stalkers to bother their prey. Email, instant messaging, and texting make for very short leashes between the stalker and the victim. Women used to be free of harassment when in school or at work, but today, the stalker sends endless messages per day and expects instant responses. This is the worst kind of instant gratification we have ever seen. This is not love. Please know that. Tanya advocated for one woman who had 152 calls in one day. Below are stories of some others.

Sara – It's Him Again

Sara's abuser was jealous and unfortunately, like so many people, she confused jealousy with love.

It must be love because he constantly checks up on me. He loves me so much that he texts me to find out where I am and where I am going. But sometimes she asked herself, *Is it too much?*

He constantly harassed her, asking her when she was coming home and who she was with. Sara interpreted it as caring and loving. *After all, he just wants to know where I am, right?*

Wrong. He only wanted to keep track of her to control her.

This is NOT love. LOVE is trusting.

Jodi – Stalked at College

Jodi, a college student, started dating a guy named Jim. She liked being with him, but when they were apart, he constantly sent her text messages, emails, and voicemails. After breaking up with him, she was surprised to see him still stalking her. Unwilling to accept the break, he even threatened suicide.

Is he trying to make me feel guilty? I'm sure he won't actually follow through.

His stalking behavior continued as he showed up at parties, causing embarrassing scenes because of his drinking and his jealousy. Someone new came into her life and they both received threatening texts from Jim. Jodi couldn't concentrate and eventually she sought out a restraining order, dropped out of college, and moved back home to regain her thoughts and sense of self.

❧

This is NOT love.
LOVE is letting go when it's over.

❧

Paula – Professionals Not Exempt

After one of Tanya's presentations, Paula asked her a question we have heard several times: "Can a professional like me be abused? My boyfriend is constantly calling and texting me. He always wants to know who I am hanging out with and what I am doing. So, is this abuse?"

It's like he wants to, and needs to, know my every move. Isn't he supposed to trust me? It seems he doesn't respect me. Why doesn't he seem to understand my need for space?

Yes, professionals can be stalked too. It can happen to anyone.

❧

This is NOT love.
LOVE believes in space and equality.

❧

Tanya – Where Were You?

After Nicole was killed, I fell into a committed relationship. It was another day after court and Richard and I wanted to have a BBQ. I drove to the store to get ketchup and mustard and a few things.

On the way to the parking structure, my neighbor Debbie needed a shoulder to lean on. Debbie was experiencing the same tragedy because her daughter had been murdered and we spent a few minutes together before walking into the store.

When I returned home, it was as if my ex had stored up all of his energy from the tip of his toes to the top of his head to explode when I walked in. In anger, he yelled, "Where were you? It's been 45 minutes and the store is only 5 minutes away. Who were you talking to? How come it took you so long?" I knew nothing I said would calm him down. He wouldn't believe me anyway.

Why is he acting like this? Why is he unwilling to share me with anyone?

He claimed he had called the hospital, police station, and my family but I checked and he had never called. *Why does he lie to me?*

This is NOT love.
LOVE is unselfish, truthful, and kind.

Real Love Is...
——— Trusting and Loving ———

"Babe, just wanted to remind you that I'm going out with my friends tonight. Should be back around 10pm, but you never know — we might be having too much fun to come home." Anne winked at John before kissing him goodbye.

He squeezed her close and said, "Yes, I know how it is when you ladies get together. Have fun... And just let me know by text or something if it looks like you'll be later, okay?" He tapped her nose before she turned to leave.

"You got it." She nearly skipped toward the door. *I love hanging out with my girlfriends!*

Just as she expected, she and the girls were having way too much fun at 10pm to call it a night and when she dug her phone out, there was a text from him: "I love you. Hope you're having fun."

She smiled, feeling her heart swell with gratitude that he supported her much-needed girl time, and texted back: "I love you too. And we are having fun. Looks like we'll be at least another hour or so. I'll let you know if it will be later...xoxoxox..."

Two seconds later, he responded, "Glad you're having fun. xoxoxo."

Awwww...I can't wait to get home and plant one on his face.

Two hours later, she sent a quick text before pulling out: "Be home in 20 minutes...I love you."

Again, just a moment later: "Yay. Kisses waiting..."

I love it that he misses me when I'm gone — that he trusts and loves me.

Jealous Stalker
—— QUESTIONS AND TIPS ——

 Questions:

1. Do you feel like you are walking on eggshells?

2. Do you ignore your inner voice that is suggesting that his behavior is excessive?

3. Does he control where you go, who you are with, and what you do?

4. Does he check up on you all the time?

5. What are 3 things you can do today to build your self-confidence and esteem?

Overall Tips:

1. Encourage yourself every day. Do one thing that brings you happiness and joy.

2. If your friend is going through it, don't try to fix it. Just be there, and don't try to fix her or the relationship. Listen. Listen. Listen.

3. Tell yourself that you believe that this is happening because this awareness will save your life.

4. If your friend tells you a story about this abuse, tell her that you believe her because she needs your support.

5. If you are walking on eggshells, now may be the time to re-evaluate the relationship.

6. 800-799-SAFE — Call for help.

2

Mind Game Player

The mind game player tells his girlfriend what to do to please him. He tells her to change her hairstyle, or her clothes, or the way she speaks. When she changes for him, he changes his mind. It isn't about her appearance or the way she speaks. It is about control. She is the marionette and he is the puppet master.

Vicki – I Know What is Best for You

Vicki's guy bought her clothes and insisted she change her hairstyle. "You would look so much better," he would tell her. "Listen to me, Babe. I know what is best for you." But, he couldn't seem to make up his mind.

First, he wanted her hair curly. *I really like it that he cares enough about me to suggest things about my appearance.* Then he thought it should be short, so she cut it off. Suggesting it would be cuter if straight, she went back to straight. Vicki was terribly confused!

It wasn't just her hair. He went with her to buy her clothes. Whatever she chose, he didn't like. He insisted on totally different styles. *I am happy that he wants me to look nice.* Later, he bought her clothes and took them to her. In every aspect of their lives, she obligingly did what he wanted even though he continued to change his mind.

Is this about my clothes or style? Why does he change his mind so much? Is this just about control? Why does he want to change me so badly anyway? Shouldn't he like me for who I am?

❡

This is NOT love. LOVE accepts and encourages individuality.

❡

Tanya – Justifying Her Professional Growth

I had a boyfriend who verbalized how proud he was of me. He was so supportive in so many ways, but I began to question his authenticity when someone drew my attention to a strange pattern. It was one of those chaotic times when I had a ton of things going on, and whenever I had to leave for a speaking engagement, there was usually a fight. This happened early in my relationship, so I was not seeing clearly and I didn't have any significant boundaries at that time because I was still so young mentally.

I don't recall what the fights were about, but I do remember sharing them with my mom, who brought to my attention that every time I had to leave for speaking, there was an argument of some sort. Even when I had networking events to go to, there were initially words of support, but then ridicule: "Do you really need to go to all of these?"

I always felt like I had to justify what I was doing. I remember an evening that I was speaking to a local women's group and came home reserved because many times when I was elated, he would put me down. So, I began to keep the excitement to myself.

This is NOT love. LOVE celebrates success authentically.

Karen – She Used to Have Fun

Karen, more than anything, loved to have fun, singing with the performers at Western concerts, dancing, applauding easily and "playing," as she called it. Surrounded by friends, she smiled often and laughed out loud.

Tired of dating guys who never read a book or had an idea, intelligent Ken was a welcome change. But, soon after they started dating, he changed: her noise was met with frowns and admonitions to grow up; her desire to go to concerts was met with judgment that they were silly and a waste of time.

I like so many things about him. I'll just change. It's okay. I really want to please him.

When her cousin complained that he had changed her, Karen told her cousin to mind her own business.

This is NOT love. LOVE accepts unique personalities.

Katy — She Couldn't Do Anything Right

Katy's mother had been married 3 times, her father 7 times, and she wasn't about to be like them so she set out to be the perfect wife. *If I do everything right, he won't leave me.*

The ideal compliant target for Carl, Katy was bright and joyful. But it didn't take long for Carl to downplay her intelligence and crush her joy.

They married quickly and he made his expectations clear.

He complains about everything. I do one thing and he says I should have done something else. I study and he complains about quick meals. I grocery shop and he says I should have been cleaning. I can't seem to do anything right. His expectations were so precise that he demanded the mail always be put in one place and screamed at her when it wasn't done.

Ignoring her emotional needs, robbing her of her sense of well-being, her self-esteem, and her joy, he even withheld sex over minor infractions.

This is NOT love. LOVE builds you up.

Real Love Is...
———— Making Everyone Happy ————

"Ok," said Steve. "I think I have this figured out. Correct me if I'm wrong, but I think we can do one of three things: go on vacation, put the tax refund in the bank, or pay for the swimming lessons for the kids."

Cathy listened carefully to Steve and then threw her arms around his neck. "How did I ever get so lucky to have a husband like you? Josh would have insisted on the vacation and acted like a two-year-old if he didn't get it." She shook her head as she remembered how her previous fiancée had constantly manipulated her to get what he wanted with no regard for her or her desires. She always felt so beat down and promised that she would never be in that position again…or put someone else in it.

I so appreciate Steve.

He smiled at her, hiding his irritation at the thought of anyone mistreating this beautiful woman, before he continued, "It's hard to decide. I know you want the vacation, but I'm not sure this is the right time financially."

"I know. I wish it was different, but we need to be practical," she said with true disappointment in her voice.

Steve saw the disappointment and wondered out loud if there was a way to do the practical thing and make her happy. "How about this? We pay for the swimming lessons and, at the end of the summer, we take a weekend trip with the family to celebrate the new swimmers. We could get a place with a good pool and have lots of fun. And, we wouldn't have to worry about the kids drowning!"

"Great idea!" she exclaimed as her face brightened. "Thank you for taking such good care to make everyone in our family happy."

Mind Game Player
—————— QUESTIONS AND TIPS ——————

 Questions:

1. Have you ever changed your personality, hobbies, or appearance for him?

2. Do you feel better or worse about yourself when he makes a suggestion for you to change?

3. Do you find yourself justifying his behavior and making excuses for him?

4. Does he make you feel that you aren't "good enough"?

5. Is your whole identity wrapped up in him? Are his friends the only friends that you have as a couple?

 Overall Tips:

1. Encourage yourself every day. Do one thing that brings you happiness and joy.

2. If your friend is going through it, don't try to fix it. Just be there, and don't try to fix her or the relationship. Listen. Listen. Listen.

3. Tell yourself that you believe that this is happening because this awareness will save your life.

4. If your friend tells you a story about this abuse, tell her that you believe her because she needs your support.

5. If you are walking on eggshells, now may be the time to re-evaluate the relationship.

6. 800-799-SAFE — Call for help.

3

Isolator

The abuser begins to isolate his victim from family and friends, creating a type of prison for just the two of them. This abuser takes away her independence and makes her 100% dependent on him. The victim doesn't realize that isolating a person is one of the first and most dangerous beginning signs of a violent relationship. The prison is not only smaller, it is filled with name-calling and criticism, which are a part of a violent relationship. This abuse affects the inner soul. He may even prevent her from going to work or going to school. In some cases, the woman even has to ask permission to go anywhere.

Susan – He Created a Prison

Susan's abuser began to isolate her, separating her from her friends and family. *He loves me so much that he wants to be with me all the time. He really cares about me. He wants to protect me from the people that I have problems with.*

Spreading false rumors and lies about what her friends and family were saying about her were the things he did to keep her away from other people. *Sometimes it feels like a prison,* she thought.

❦

This is NOT love. LOVE is inclusive.

❦

Tanya — The Prison was Getting Smaller

It's easier to isolate you if you live with him, right? Richard had me move in with him even after knowing each other only a short time. He knew my house was crowded and crazy, so he offered, "I have a place for you in my condo. I will make room for you. You can have my room with the master closet." I took it. It sounded great ... at the time. But, that was the beginning of me getting stuck.

Richard worked evenings so I would spend time at my family's home. We moved closer to them, which caused even more problems. Eventually, he said, "I don't want you spending time with your family in the evenings. I don't want you to be with friends, especially your college roommate, Jon."

What is he so worried about?

The prison was getting smaller. "And, if you're having coffee with your sisters at the local depot and their boyfriends show up, I expect you to get up and leave because I will not have my girlfriend known as the slut around town."

❦

This is NOT love. LOVE allows you to enjoy your friends and family.

❦

Karen – Ignoring the Red Flag

During the wedding preparations, Ken demanded that Karen's friend Sheila be kicked out of the wedding party because she had gossiped, which Ken found unacceptable.

I've been friends with Sheila for a long time and I haven't known Ken all that long. I don't think what Sheila did was so bad, but it upset Ken. I really want to marry him so I guess I have to do what he says. Why should I have to lose my best friend because he is upset?

After the wedding, Karen's cousin, Shirley, tried to talk to Karen. "He's changing you and you aren't the same person anymore. You were Student Body President, for Heaven's sake, and now you just do whatever he says." When Shirley told their aunt, Ken demanded that the aunt choose between Karen and her cousin. Surprise! The aunt chose Shirley, shutting Karen out of the family circle.

Ken's goal of isolating Karen was achieved as he found more and more ways to isolate her from friends and family.

♥

This is NOT love. LOVE respects your choice of friends.

♥

Rosa – Snuck Off to College

Growing up in a happy Hispanic family, Rosa wanted to create the same thing for her husband and children. But, it didn't seem to develop as she had pictured it. Her husband said she couldn't drive because he needed the only car for work and, besides, she had a growing number of children to take care of.

41

He played poker and drank beer with his friends but wouldn't babysit so she could spend time with her friends. *I'm kind of lonely. I miss my friends.*

Finally, when her children were in school, she simply had to do something for herself so she snuck off to the local community college to take some classes.

If he finds out, he'll have a fit but I simply have to be around other people. I know I'm taking a terrible chance. Rosa snuck her way out of isolation.

Fortunately, it didn't lead to physical violence, but she was one of the lucky ones.

♥

This is NOT love. LOVE unselfishly shares.

♥

Real Love Is...
———— Spending Time with Family ————

"Honey, my dad is alone this weekend. Let's invite him to dinner and spoil him a bit," said Mary, her face lighting up as she thought about treating her dad to some family time. She and her husband Don regularly hosted family get-togethers for holidays, birthdays, and other celebrations, and she loved every minute of it.

"Great idea!" Don responded and offered to call and invite him.

As Mary watched her two favorite men interact with each other across the dinner table, her heart felt full and happy. Don was the perfect host and genuinely happy to spend time with Mary's dad. They had fun, talking about football in the fall and who was going to win.

"Thank you, Honey," said Mary, as she snuggled into his arm on the couch. "Dad had such a good time and we did too. I love you, Don."

"Anything for you, Dear," and he meant it.

Isolator

———— QUESTIONS AND TIPS ————

 Questions:

1. Does he seem to want you to himself all the time?

2. Does he criticize your friends and family and try to keep you away from them? Does he become angry if you see them?

3. Do you make up excuses not to spend time with friends?

4. Do you sometimes feel like you are in a prison?

5. Do you feel lonely because you don't see your family and friends anymore?

 Overall Tips:

1. Encourage yourself every day. Do one thing that brings you happiness and joy.

2. If your friend is going through it, don't try to fix it. Just be there, and don't try to fix her or the relationship. Listen. Listen. Listen.

3. Tell yourself that you believe that this is happening because this awareness will save your life.

4. If your friend tells you a story about this abuse, tell her that you believe her because she needs your support.

5. If you are walking on eggshells, now may be the time to re-evaluate the relationship.

6. 800-799-SAFE — Call for help.

4

Emotional Robber

The emotional robber tells the victim how to feel. He robs her of her true and genuine feelings. Nobody has the right to tell you how to feel. That is your truth. If you are sad, be sad. If you are mad, be mad. Just vent appropriately.

Karen – Straighten Up and Be Happy

Karen was a bright, enthusiastic, energetic, creative and verbal girl. As she got older, she remained that way until she met Ken who told her it was immature or silly to feel a certain way. Whatever she felt, it wasn't right.

Only a month after Karen's father and stepfather died within 36 hours of each other, Karen and Ken went to a surprise birthday party for one of Ken's friends. While they were playing games, Karen sat down in the den because she felt terribly sad and didn't feel like a party. Ken came in and asked, "What are you doing?" When Karen told him, he said, "This is a party. Straighten up and be happy."

She sat a moment longer thinking, *I hate him.* She straightened up that night but divorced him later.

❧

This is NOT love. LOVE accepts your feelings and comforts you.

❧

Tanya — Get Over It!

I recall coming home one day after spending 8 hours listening to my sister's murder trial. I was absolutely exhausted and began to cry, and was met with cruelty, "It's been almost a year; get over it. Go to your room." Well, I did. I just didn't want to hear it anymore.

Going to my room does not feel so bad. It was quiet.

❧

This is NOT love. LOVE is patient and tender.

❧

Janice — Husband or Bully?

Janice grew up being emotional and a little over-dramatic, almost exploding when she told stories to her friends.

Her husband constantly insulted and demeaned her. He told her she was stupid and her emotional outbursts were childish. When she was happy, he said she should be more serious; when sad, he said she had nothing to be sad about; and when she was reflective, he accused her of brooding.

I love my husband but he just doesn't accept me. He constantly criticizes me, disrespects me, and yells at me. It's almost like he's a bully.

Not restricted to the schoolyard, bullies can be in our homes and Janice lived with one. It was too hard and pretty soon, she stopped being overly dramatic and eventually stopped "feeling" altogether.

❧

This is NOT love. LOVE cares about your feelings.

❧

Sally — You Have to Cry Some Other Time

Sally had been married to Larry for several years when her adult son from her first marriage was murdered. After the funeral, everyone tried to settle back into their routine, but Sally would cry when she went to bed. Having worked all day and fulfilled duties at home, bedtime seemed like the only time to cry. Larry would jump up and down and say, "Stop that! You have to cry some other time. I have to go to work tomorrow."

I have to go to work too. My heart is broken, and I don't know when I'm supposed to cry.

She suppressed her emotions, and six months later she was in a mental hospital. *What I really want to do is walk into the ocean and just keep on walking.*

Today she seldom cries. She didn't even cry when her mother and her husband died.

❧

This is NOT love. LOVE cuddles
you while you cry.

❧

49

Real Love Is...
——— Letting You Feel Your Feelings ———

Barbara looked so sad that Tom just had to go give her a big hug. "I know it's hard to lose someone so dear to you, Honey," he said.

"Thanks, Babe, I wish I felt differently but every time I think of her, I just hate it that I can't see her." Barbara snuggled into his embrace, appreciating his wonderful support.

"I know. I miss her too," he whispered into her hair, feeling her tears wet his shirt.

Barbara was feeling the warmth of Tom's body and it was easing the pain.

I'm so glad I don't have to be strong for him when I feel so sad. He lets me be real about my feelings.

Emotional Robber
——— QUESTIONS AND TIPS ———

 Questions:

1. Does he tell you how to feel?

2. Does he belittle your opinions and feelings?

3. Have your friends commented on how your once bubbly personality isn't so bubbly anymore and you seem to have been replaced by a withdrawn, quiet person with few opinions, ideas, or feelings?

4. Do you avoid giving your opinion in order to avoid conflict and keep the peace?

5. Do you ignore your inner voice that says, "Of course, I have a right to feel however I actually feel and to have opinions?"

 Overall Tips:

1. Encourage yourself every day. Do one thing that brings you happiness and joy.

2. If your friend is going through it, don't try to fix it. Just be there, and don't try to fix her or the relationship. Listen. Listen. Listen.

3. Tell yourself that you believe that this is happening because this awareness will save your life.

4. If your friend tells you a story about this abuse, tell her that you believe her because she needs your support.

5. If you are walking on eggshells, now may be the time to re-evaluate the relationship.

6. 800-799-SAFE — Call for help.

5

Money Monger

The money monger's goal is to put his victim into financial isolation. Traditionally, men made money and women didn't, so if the husband didn't want to "share," the woman was very dependent upon him. Today, it is perhaps more obvious. Some women who make an excellent salary can still fall prey to the money monger and become financially dependent on him.

The misperception of our society is that domestic violence only happens to those in low socioeconomic households. The truth is it happens to the rich as well.

Diane — Where Would You Go?

Diane was a wealthy woman, or perhaps we should say that Diane was married to a wealthy man. He kept her in financial isolation by keeping all the money in his name and giving her an allowance.

When she considered leaving him, he responded, "Where would you go? I have all the money. You want to leave all this and put our kids on the streets? I give you cars, furs, getaways, diamonds. You live in a 20,000 square foot house. You'll be ostracized by the other women."

I'm miserable, but I have to stay for the kids. I don't want to take all of this luxury away from them. I don't want to take them away from their friends. I'm afraid of leaving. I'll just put up the front and pretend I'm happy.

Surrendering, Diane stayed because of the kids, not knowing that by staying, she was raising a potential victim and/or a potential abuser.

This is NOT love. LOVE is generous.

Tanya – Financially Trapped

Richard maxed out my credit cards to ensure that I could not spend any more money with them. He paid bills with my credit cards. He put bills in my name giving me bad credit and nowhere to turn. He hid credit card bills, telling me everything was okay. I trusted him with the finances but it made me dependent on him.

Richard would buy me lavish gifts, but at times we couldn't even afford a hamburger. One year I received a tennis bracelet for Christmas and that is when I began to question him. I later discovered he went into my mutual fund and that is where I found out what he was doing.

Oh my goodness! He is stealing my money!

I was financially trapped and when I finally left him, I had nothing. My credit cards were gone. He had forged 13 checks against my mutual fund and ruined my credit. He was my financial advisor who did not have permission to enter my account. But somehow, he schmoozed his way into it.

One night he came over to my parent's house and cried at the kitchen table, "I will never leave you with this financial obligation." After that evening, I never saw a dime or him.

❤

This is NOT love. LOVE is truthful.

❤

Sally – No Coca Cola after Choir

Sally never had any money when she was with Don. He worked and got his paycheck and did whatever he wanted, including buying fishing equipment and taking flying lessons.

I hate that I never have my own money. He thinks all the money is "his," and I don't even have enough money to go out for a Coca Cola after choir practice. I know I can't make it without him or on my own.

When her youngest son became an adult, he said that what he remembered was that Sally had 6 people and 4 animals to feed on only $25-$30 per week.

Don kept Sally poor and lacking the skills and the courage to do anything about her situation. At one time, she inherited $10,000 from a distant relative and Don took over the money, went through it quickly, and spent every cent on himself.

❤

This is NOT love. LOVE shares.

❤

Sandra – He Controlled Every Cent

A successful secretary during her first marriage, Sandra loved clothes and shoes and liked to indulge in these niceties most every payday. Things changed when she married the second time. Marrying a very successful man, she thought she would be able buy anything she wanted. He did spoil her during their engagement, but when they married, that all stopped. Ted controlled the money, made all the financial decisions, and told her, "Don't worry your pretty little head about the finances. I'll take care of all of that."

It makes me kind of nervous because he controls all the money. I guess it's okay, but my name isn't on any of the bank accounts. I wish I could go back to work. All I get is this allowance for the household expenses, and I'm starting to feel trapped.

Financial isolation was one of his goals. With no access to bank accounts or investments, and held to only a small allowance, she was literally trapped and it was fairly impossible for her to leave.

❦

This is NOT love. LOVE spoils.

❦

Real Love Is...
—— Sharing the Financial Decisions ——

"Honey, it's that time of the month again," said Patricia with a smirk. "Bill paying time."

Ken pretended to be exhausted by the mere idea, but the truth was he actually enjoyed the way they handled money. Since the beginning, they had always sat down together and planned their finances, and shuddered when they heard their friends talking about their financial couple woes.

"Alright. I'm coming, Honey," he said, giving her a big grin as he walked over to the table.

"That extra bonus really came in handy," he said. "I was going to buy a new fishing rod but I changed my mind."

"Well," replied Patricia, "I thought of a new dress for your company party, but I can wear the one from my cousin's wedding. People at the company have never seen it."

"Well, it's kind of a bummer in a way," responded Ken. "But, I have good news!"

"What is that?" asked Patricia.

"We have paid off the MasterCard, and our credit score went up a few points."

"Yippee!" Patricia squealed as she gave him a monster hug. "That's better than a new dress any day."

He squeezed her back before saying, "I'm proud of us. We are managing our money well and I love that we make the decisions together."

Money Monger
—— QUESTIONS AND TIPS ——

 Questions:

1. Has he suggested you place an asset of yours in his name?

2. Does he limit your access to your own money?

3. Does he make you account for all of the money that you spend or put you on an allowance?

4. Do you fear he will leave you if you don't let him manage the money?

5. Do you ignore your inner voice that says, "I earned this money. Why do I have to give it to him?"

 Overall Tips:

1. Encourage yourself every day. Do one thing that brings you happiness and joy.

2. If your friend is going through it, don't try to fix it. Just be there, and don't try to fix her or the relationship. Listen. Listen. Listen.

3. Tell yourself that you believe that this is happening because this awareness will save your life.

4. If your friend tells you a story about this abuse, tell her that you believe her because she needs your support.

5. If you are walking on eggshells, now may be the time to re-evaluate the relationship.

6. 800-799-SAFE — Call for help.

6

Pseudo Parent

Real parents love and nurture their children, but this abuser harms them. When a man abuses the mother of his children, he abuses them as well. They are harmed by this sad, angry, and at times violent living situation. At this point, the children can also become victims of domestic violence or grow up to become batterers themselves. While many moms believe they are staying for the betterment of their children, the truth is they are hurting their children by staying.

Penny – Children Hear Everything

Penny was so naïve when it came to her precious children.

They do not know. They were asleep upstairs. They didn't hear anything.

Not true. Penny's children heard and felt everything. They were the first ones with their little ears to the floor or wall. They felt it when Penny and their dad were fighting. Penny didn't find out that they knew until her daughter cried to her saying, "Why do you and daddy always fight?"

Penny wanted so badly to be a good parent and she tried, but the fighting harmed her little ones in ways she didn't understand.

This is NOT love. LOVE solves problems without hurting others.

Debra – Everyone Thought Kevin was a Great Guy

Debra and Kevin lived in a beautiful home with their three adolescent children and appeared to be the perfect family. Both professionals and participating in their children's lives, they were admired by friends. Everyone thought Kevin, a TV weatherman and local personality, was a great guy. Yet, behind closed doors he was totally different, yelling and verbally abusing her and the children, degrading them on a regular basis.

I'm worried about my children. I think they are being affected. They used to be super involved and now they come home and just are quiet, almost like they're walking on eggshells.

The truth was they were changing as Kevin manipulated and hurt them because he knew this would be the best way to hurt Debra.

I told my friend, but she didn't believe me. She thought I was making it up. She kept saying how funny and fun Kevin is. I know everyone likes him but he's different at home. It makes me feel so alone.

No matter how hard she tried to share her life experiences, none of her friends understood and they suggested she stick by her man. She was so alone that she sought help at a shelter support group. This helped her understand that even if she didn't want to leave for herself, she should consider leaving for her children. Members of the group understood that a mother's motivation will always be to protect her children.

This is NOT love. LOVE is encouraging.

Sally – The Cycle of Violence Continued

Don wouldn't even watch his own kids, and if he was with them for a short time, he ignored them, never interacting with them.

I have to do all the work, and I never get any credit. I try and try but if anything goes wrong, I get blamed. One of the kids got hurt and he yelled at me at the hospital in front of the other family members. He said, "If you were a good mother, this wouldn't have happened!" I was so humiliated and shamed. I didn't know what to do.

Unfortunately, their oldest son copied his father's behavior and the cycle of violence continued.

This is NOT love. LOVE connects
and empathizes.

John and Sarah – Raising a Predator and a Victim

John and Sarah fought all the time and Sarah was being emotionally abused, but their children, Sammy and Judy, were being abused as well. John directly abused the children, belittling, shaming, and bullying them.

I feel so bad when John yells at them. It's bad enough that he does it to me but to bully the children makes me sad. I don't know what to do. We love our children, but I know we don't have a perfect family life. Sometimes, I fear that Judy will grow up to be like me but I tell her to expect good treatment.

Indirectly, the harm was even more devastating. John taught Sammy that women weren't worth much and treating a woman poorly was acceptable. John taught Judy that women can be abused and then smile and serve dinner. Unfortunately, the children will follow what they experience not what they are told. Their models taught them that men can control and dominate women and women must be submissive. John and Sarah don't realize it but they are raising a potential predator and a potential victim.

This is NOT love. LOVE nurtures
and honors children.

Real Love Is...
———— Parenting With Care ————

"I'm kind of concerned about something," said Kate, a few minutes after they had dropped the kids off at her parents' house. "The other night when we were talking about money...we got a little angry at each other."

"I know," said John. "I felt bad about that because we usually do such a good job of showing respect for each other, especially in front of the children."

"I do respect you, John," Kate smiled and leaned over to give him a big smooch on his cheek.

He smiled, "Likewise, as you know...and I have an idea," John continued. "How about we have a signal that means we should continue a certain discussion when the kids aren't around?"

"Great idea," agreed Kate. "I don't want to burden them with money worries and other things they don't understand. How about if the signal is 'Car Convo,' and we'll know that it means that it's a discussion to have in the car where the kids can't hear?"

He nodded his agreement before adding, "This parenting thing is harder than I thought it would be. But, I'm glad we're figuring it out together." He reached for her hand and glanced at her. "So, 'Car Convo' it will be if it's something the kids shouldn't hear."

"Great idea," she agreed, feeling relieved about their decision.

Pseudo Parent
—— QUESTIONS AND TIPS ——

 Questions:

1. When you show love for your children, does he suggest you are spoiling them?

2. Do your children hear it when he criticizes you?

3. Have your children become numb about the abuse going on in the household?

4. Does he threaten to harm or take the children from you?

5. Do you ignore your inner voice that says, "Maybe instead of staying for my children, I should leave for their benefit?"

 Overall Tips:

1. Encourage yourself every day. Do one thing that brings you happiness and joy.

2. If your friend is going through it, don't try to fix it. Just be there, and don't try to fix her or the relationship. Listen. Listen. Listen.

3. Tell yourself that you believe that this is happening because this awareness will save your life.

4. If your friend tells you a story about this abuse, tell her that you believe her because she needs your support.

5. If you are walking on eggshells, now may be the time to re-evaluate the relationship.

6. 800-799-SAFE — Call for help.

_____

_____

_____

_____

_____

_____

_____

_____

_____

_____

_____

_____

_____

_____

_____

_____

_____

_____

7

Silent Knight

One of the most hurtful types of abusers is the silent knight. He gives his girlfriend or wife the silent treatment. This quiet abuser does not threaten. He does not lose his temper. He just withholds affection, love, and all other emotions. He remains silent until he is ready to speak. The abuse continues. While the temperature goes up, her self-esteem goes down. He is slowly stealing it from her.

Carla – Tim Withheld Affection

Carla liked Tim from the very beginning because he was so strong and sure of himself. They first met at a party, and she was just drawn to his quiet demeanor. She admired the fact that he never lost his temper, no matter what. They dated and married, and they fought. The fighting happened more and more frequently, but he never threatened or yelled at her.

I love it that he doesn't yell. My father yelled all the time and I just hated it.

71

Yet there was another side to this strong silent type. The silence wasn't just about words. It included feelings.

Sometimes though, it's hard because he doesn't tell me what he is thinking or how he is feeling. I ask him and he won't answer. Sometimes, I even doubt if he loves me.

❡

This is NOT love. LOVE shows affection.

❡

Tanya – Stealing Her Self-esteem

He didn't talk to me for three days. I was going stir crazy. I had that little hamster in my head that would not stop. I was wondering what I did wrong.

Did I say something to offend him? If so, what? Why won't you say anything?

I was so confused because I thought everything else in the relationship was going so well. I had been led to believe that whatever was wrong with the relationship was my fault. I was so apologetic, yet he still was giving me the silent treatment.

The silent knight is probably the most hurtful abuser because he does not leave physical bruises or scars. The control escalated. He slowly stole my competence.

❡

This is NOT love. LOVE communicates.

❡

Karen – Silence was His Weapon

Karen married early and was very young. Raised in a dysfunctional and noisy family, she liked Ken's quiet demeanor, not realizing that it could be harmful.

One of the most dramatic examples was when Karen invited a couple of *her* friends to dinner. When they arrived, Ken greeted them but that was the last thing he said to them. Because the other three adults were talking, it wasn't noticeable at first, but became more than evident as the evening went on.

Ken isn't talking to my friends. Why not? Maybe he isn't interested in this topic. I'll try to change it. This is so embarrassing. Not only is it not fun, it's awful. I am so ashamed.

After they left — early — she asked Ken why he hadn't said anything and his mean, self-centered response was, "I had nothing to say to them." He was punishing Karen and purposefully using silence to hurt her.

This is NOT love. LOVE appreciates your effort to entertain your friends.

Melanie – From Festive to Silent

Melanie and Leo were married for only 3 years when he started giving her bouts of the silent treatment. They had a holiday party with their closest friends and Melanie shopped, prepared, and created a festive atmosphere for all to enjoy.

When they were done cleaning, Leo became very silent. He would not engage in any conversation and even when they were getting ready for bed, the energy was uncomfortable for her. He did not engage in any intimacy and, in fact, shrugged her off when she leaned over to kiss him. Melanie began going through scenarios in her mind because they had such a nice evening, so she could not understand what had happened. Any questions that she asked, he would not answer nor acknowledge.

What did I do wrong? Did I throw a bad party? Did I say something wrong?

Melanie slowly lost herself after this event, and Leo never explained why he gave her the silent treatment.

On her birthday, she went to her parent's home to pick up her present, which was two miles away. They had plans to go somewhere so she wasn't going to be long, but she stayed longer than anticipated. It was her special day so she thought nothing of it. *So, we will be a few minutes late,* she thought. When she pulled into their apartment complex, he was awaiting her, in the car, car on, door opened. All he said was, "Get in." He did not talk to her for the three-hour drive to visit with his family.

♡

This is NOT love.
LOVE communicates feelings.

♡

Real Love Is...
—Sharing, Even When It's Uncomfortable—

"I don't want to talk about it," said David. When he looked up, he saw Stephie sitting calmly, waiting.

"Okay, I know. Let's talk about it. I'm kinda upset with you," David started quietly after taking a nice deep breath. "I don't mind you going out with your mom. In fact, I wouldn't have it any other way. But, when you are late, especially *this late,* it's really hard on me. It feels like you don't respect me enough to call. So, I'm mad. And then I get worried. This time, it was so late, I actually called hospitals. I know you probably don't mean to disrespect me or make me mad, but that's how I feel."

"Oh, my," responded Stephie. "I had no idea. I'm really sorry that I didn't call to let you know that we were running so late." She paused and put her hand on his. "Thank you so much for telling me. I love you so much. I would never hurt you or make you worry on purpose. I'll do better."

Silent Knight
—— QUESTIONS AND TIPS ——

 Questions:

1. Does he ignore you and withhold affection?

2. Does he refuse to answer when you ask him a question?

3. Do you feel badly about yourself when he goes quiet on you?

4. Do you apologize too much and too often?

5. Do you ignore your inner voice that says, "I deserve a companion who participates with me in the dialogue of life"?

 Overall Tips:

1. Encourage yourself every day. Do one thing that brings you happiness and joy.

2. If your friend is going through it, don't try to fix it. Just be there, and don't try to fix her or the relationship. Listen. Listen. Listen.

3. Tell yourself that you believe that this is happening because this awareness will save your life.

4. If your friend tells you a story about this abuse, tell her that you believe her because she needs your support.

5. If you are walking on eggshells, now may be the time to re-evaluate the relationship.

6. 800-799-SAFE — Call for help.

Conclusion:
Where It Can End

Dear Reader,

Here we are at the end of our book and, if you're like most of the people we talk to about *The Seven Characters*, you may be feeling a mix of emotions and asking yourself some big questions.

We know that what happened in the courtyard in Brentwood doesn't have to happen, but it does happen…all too often. And our purpose in writing this book was to try to prevent it from happening to you, your sisters, or your friends. We want you to know that you deserve true love — love that nurtures you, encourages your dreams, supports your goals, and most of all, respects you and doesn't try to control and overpower you.

Domestic violence starts with one or more of these Seven Characters — with stalking, silence, and put-downs. It isolates you socially and financially. It manipulates your mind. It disrespects your wishes, takes away your rights, dashes your dreams, and erases your hopes. Leaving you with a little lone white flag of surrender.

The Seven Characters of Abuse, or non-physical abuse, can be isolated behaviors or part of the escalation of domestic abuse that becomes physical battering.

If you're dealing with isolated behaviors, you still need to decide if you can or should live with this lack of respect, and if you want to risk the good chance that it will become physical in the future.

If the abuse has become physical, your decision is both easier...and harder. It is easier because it's obvious when someone hits you that it is wrong and harder because now, safety is the crucial issue. Is it safer to stay where you are being hit or safer to get away?

As you contemplate your situation and begin to make decisions, we beg you to be overly cautious and stay safe:

Keep the book in a safe place, even giving it away if you are afraid he might find it.

When you use the Internet, please do it safely, perhaps even using a safe computer rather the one in your home. You don't want him to get in and find out that you've been looking for help (to get away from him) online.

When you make phone calls for information or help, you will want to protect those calls from being detected, using a phone that can't be traced through phone bills. In fact, getting a separate cell phone for you to dial in emergencies is a really good idea.

When you tell a friend, make sure it is one you can trust.

If you decide to leave your relationship, you will likely face the following questions and we want to support you by sharing a bit more about our own journey of answering those questions:

- *What* makes me stay?
- *What* will motivate me to leave?
- *Where* should I go?
- *Who* will help me to understand and *How* will I do it safely?

What Made Me Stay?

Tanya

I was alone during the time of my sister's murder trial. I needed a shoulder. My sisters and parents had grandkids to nurture and take care of. I did not. I needed someone to love and to love me back.

I did all I could to make him happy. I compromised my values just to have someone in my life. I thought life would be easier, and it was for a short while. But slowly, my esteem was taken, my confidence robbed.

So, I stayed because I did not want to be alone and I thought if I just did what I needed to do to keep peace, I might as well do it.

Carolyn

10! Yes, the number ten. My mother was married 3 times and my father was married 7 times. My desired number was 1. I wanted to be married once and once only, and I was willing to put up with a lot in order to stay married.

That's just part of marriage, I thought.

I became sad, but stayed. The sadness increased, but I stayed. The sadness was accompanied by fear, pain, and anger, but I stayed despite my Silent Knight.

What Motivated Me to Leave?

Tanya

One day, while I was unpacking in our new apartment, my mom noticed how tense and skinny I was. She questioned it, but I put her off because I still wasn't ready to leave.

Soon after that, I began to realize that he was lying to me. He said we didn't have any money, yet he was buying me a car and a bracelet. Later, I found out that he had used my money to buy me these things.

Finally, I knew I needed to get out. It was a visceral feeling, a sign that I was not happy, and I was sick and tired of being unhappy. I knew deep inside that it was time to make a change, but I was waiting for the "call" to do it.

We were at a business dinner when I got that "call" and my gut told me to get up and leave. My body was leaving and my mind was following. He followed me and asked what I was doing. I told him I was leaving and he said, "Okay, see you at home."

I wasn't going home. I left everything behind, including my iguana.

Carolyn

I was finally motivated to leave when I realized that although I was afraid of being lonely in an apartment by myself, I was lonelier in that house.

There is nothing lonelier than being in a house with a man who is withdrawing more and more into his silent shell.

I certainly contributed too. It simply was an unhealthy and unequal relationship.

But, I was afraid of taking care of myself financially. I had moved from my parents' home to my 'marriage home' and I had never lived alone before.

But the future held promise and I was optimistic about discovering the true me and what I wanted. I remember telling my counselor that I could now have pink pillows if I wanted.

Finally, the fear of the future was less than the sadness of the present, so I ran away from home.

Each of you beautiful women will decide for yourself when you have had enough. Hopefully, we have helped to clarify behaviors that are not loving and further helped you identify what love is.

Where Did I Go?

Tanya	*Carolyn*
Thankfully, I had my family to turn to. (Sadly, many do not.)	Most women in this situation need to be extremely careful in order to remain safe.
My relationship never got to the point where I was concerned for my safety, but had I stayed, I do believe it would have escalated.	That was not the case with me.
	Since I had no reason to be afraid of retribution, I moved close by so my child could visit me on weekends.
I had nothing but my clothes and photo albums. I had no money and tons of debt.	Before long, I got a larger apartment and she moved in with me.
But, I had my safety and was building my esteem back.	
Get out SAFELY.	
Call 1-800-799-SAFE.	
You must do it safely.	
DO NOT pick up and leave.	

1-800-799-SAFE will direct you to services, which will help you make a plan including where to go.

Who Will Help Me to Understand *How* to Do It Safely?

The wonderful people suggested by 1-800-799-SAFE are there to support your efforts to find safety, calm, and eventually positive love. The first goal is SAFETY, and a safety plan is key.

You will not feel alone and you will see that there are many women and kids who are experiencing the EXACT same situation: "Same guy, different face."

Why is Simple.

Love is not control and power, and leaving is logical when the behavior is not loving. The single most important goal of the book has been to clarify this question, which is to emphasize that when we are not treated with respect, love, and nurturing, it may be time to leave.

We hope that you will listen to the little voice inside. It is usually right. Christopher Reeve once said, *"I think we all have a little voice inside us that will guide us…if we shut out all the noise and clutter from our lives and listen to the voice, it will tell us the right thing to do."*

Thank you for the opportunity to spend a few hours with you. We hope you have found this book to be enlightening and helpful.

Our greatest hope for you is that you come to a place where you can learn to love your life and yourself once again. To come to a place where when you describe yourself, you can easily say, "I am loved by a person who treats me with RESPECT, kindness, encouragement, and support — someone who cherishes me."

We believe you deserve that type of person and love in your life!

Huge hugs!

Tanya and Carolyn

Hopeful Resources

There is hope. Although this topic may seem depressing, there is hope that individuals will stop domestic violence because they stop being in a relationship that is unhealthy. Women can cease to be victims. It is possible to stop domestic violence and we must do so. Let's get into action and find solutions.

The exciting thing is that the dirty little secret is much less of a secret than it was previously. And the causes and solutions are more well-known as well.

Immediate Assistance for Victims

A Note of Caution:

Please be careful with these numbers, especially if you are worried about an angry partner finding them. You might want to put them in a safe place or you can put them under anonymous names.

If you or someone you know is experiencing domestic or intimate partner violence, call the **National Domestic Violence Hotline** at **1-800-799-SAFE** for immediate assistance. Representatives are available 24 hours a day, seven days a week. This is an anonymous phone number in 140 languages.

Write down the numbers for your local agencies in case you need them:

Police _____

Emergency Police: __911_____

Shelters _____

Coalitions _____

churches _____

For Victims: Overcoming the Reluctance to Act

Denial

There is a tremendous reluctance to act because there is great denial. We agree with Dave Navarro, of The Joyful Heart, who stated it so well, *"We are trying to raise awareness so people can get help or even assess their situation. The denial is so thick that sometimes it's hard to get a grasp of one's self within a conflict. But if someone can see themselves in the campaign, maybe they can reach out for help."* Our book humbly has the same goal — to break through the denial by sharing stories of victims of non-physical abuse.

"Maybe There Isn't Really a Problem..."

If you answered yes to more than a few of the questions at the end of the chapters, you need to ask your innermost self if you have a problem. Only you can truly answer that question. The first step to solving any problem is admitting it. You can continue to deny it, minimize it, and ignore it. But, please understand that it will get worse.

"Maybe It Was Only One Time or Just a Few Times..."

Abuse has many forms including intimidation, threats, isolation, financial isolation and all the things discussed in this book. In all honesty, if these things occur often, they are apt to escalate, not disappear. And, unfortunately, physical violence often follows emotional control. Physical violence, perhaps the last tactic aside from murder, is just one step away from the threats, power, and control.

"Perhaps I Should Learn More About The Problem..."

For some of you, this book will be enough for you to realize that you are a victim. Others will want to become more knowledgeable about emotional domestic violence. There are many excellent articles, books, and websites. The Resource Section will help you begin your search.

"I Feel I Should Stay for the Children..."

That is a myth. You should seriously consider leaving *for* the children.

When you stay, the children can be harmed significantly.

Sometimes, the abuser harms them before they are born. In fact, the March of Dimes reports that battering during pregnancy is the leading cause of birth defects and infant mortality. Most times, they harm them after they are born. When a man abuses the mother of his children, he abuses them as well. They are harmed by this sad and angry living situation, and the children also become victims of domestic violence.

There is a sad irony of staying for the sake of the children. Sometimes, children even try to "protect mommy from being hurt" and in turn get hurt themselves. They are physically abused. As they get older, some fight back and then they pay the price. 63% of young men between the ages of 11 and 20 who are serving time in prison for homicide have killed their mother's abuser. And other young boys become young men who abuse their girlfriends and wives.

The results do not have to be so dramatic, but it is a fact that all children from a domestic violence home are emotionally hurt and have trouble with their future lives.

This makes it all the more critical to get out of those homes.

"I thought that abuse only occurred in poor, uneducated and minority families..."

Abuse occurs in all income levels, professions, religions, cultures, educational levels and races. You are not the only one.

"Maybe I Should Just Leave..."

Don't just pick up and leave. Tanya's sister, Nicole, did that and look what happened. This is a potential murder case, not just a divorce or a separation. It must be done safely.

You will know when it is time to leave but you need professional help. Here are three ways to get that help:

First, you must create a Safety Plan.*

Secondly, all women can call 1-800-799-SAFE.

And, finally, if you live in Southern California, Tanya is always here to help you find support, shelter, and safety. You may contact Tanya through www.TanyaBrown.net or via email: Tanya@TanyaBrown.net

More on the Safety Plan *

Safety needs to be your number one concern when you are thinking about leaving. As mentioned before, Tanya's sister picked up, moved less than 2 miles away, got a divorce, and ended up dead. These are not divorce cases; these have to be looked at as potential murder cases. Our intention is not to scare you, but to help you realize that YOU HAVE TO DO THIS THE RIGHT WAY. So, here are tips that can get you safe and keep you safe (adapted by: www.domesticviolence.org/personalized-safety-plan)

- Have important numbers: 911, shelters, and confidants
- Tell one or two trusted people about the abuse. Ask them to call the police if they hear or witness things.
- Take the time to create an exit strategy. Visualize yourself in the situation to help you do this.

- Think how you might leave. Take the trash out, walk the dog, go to the store, leave when they are at work and then not come back and go to the police or go to your safe house or other place you could go to.
- Do not go into any rooms where there are items that can be used as weapons.
- Prepare a get-away bag and ask someone you trust to keep it for you and to help you temporarily with money.
  » Medicine
  » Things for the kids (if any)
    Blankets
    Toys
    Clothes
    Bottles etc.
  » Phone numbers
  » Important Documents
    Birth certificates
    School records
    Medical records
    Banking items
    Insurance documents
    Mortgage/rental agreements
    Restraining orders
      – Give to workplace/police/school/church and anywhere else you visit.
- Social Security Card
- Driving License I.D. card
- Address book
- Jewelry heirlooms memorabilia

» **NO credit cards! They will trace it.**
» Keys (house, work, car)
» Clothes
» Hygiene items

WARNING: Abusers try to control their victim's lives. When abusers feel a loss of control – like when victims try to leave them – the abuse often gets worse. Take special care when you leave. Keep being careful even after you have left.

This section on personalized safety planning is adapted from the Metro Nashville Police Department's personalized safety plan.

For Friends and Family: How You Can Help

It's hard for the victim to leave but harder if friends and families don't understand. As her friend or relative, it is important for you to understand the problem and the best way to help her.

"Why Does She Stay?"

Some women stay because they are <u>ashamed</u>. They are embarrassed. They don't want people to know that they are being abused.

Some women stay because they are <u>hopeful</u>. They hope that things will get better. They did not marry a monster. The monster revealed himself as time went on. Hope is the one thing that they hold on to. They hope that one day the person they married will come back.

Some women stay because they have <u>surrendered</u>. One woman said, "We have food on the table; we have a roof over our heads; we have clothes on our backs. I can put up with the abuse so my children have these things. It's not that bad. As long as I keep my mouth SHUT, our lives will be easier. If I just listen to him and do what I am told, nothing will happen."

And, ultimately they all stay because they are <u>afraid</u>. You might stay too if you had heard the words, "If you leave, I will kill you!" or "If I can't have you, nobody can." She knows his temper so she is frightened.

There are great risks in leaving: Women who leave their batterers are at a 75% greater risk of being killed by the batterer than those who stay. Nicole was one of those victims who left, felt freedom, and then was murdered.

"What Can I Do About It?"

It may be time to speak up. You don't have to wait for her to come to you. We previously quoted Christopher Reeve regarding the little voice that tells us what to do. If the little voice tells you something is wrong, don't ignore it. If your friend or family member is being abused, you probably suspect that it is happening.

You may be hesitating because you feel it's none of your business. As a friend or family member, it is loving to show that you care and are brave enough to express your concern. Simply ask if there is a problem, if something is wrong.

Open the door to conversation if you suspect it but she has not yet told you. Tread lightly and do not force the issue. But find some way to start the dialogue. You might tell her you heard about the NFL player or something on the news about increased awareness. Let her arrive on her own time. For now, just be there with her. She will share more when she is ready. Be there for her and let her know you're there to help, but don't scare her away.

Don't judge or blame her. Don't accuse or criticize her. The abuser criticizes her enough. Just listen to her.

Don't pressure her or tell her what to do. Don't give advice. Support her decisions. Listen and validate. As Tanya says, "Listen! Listen! Listen!"

Don't place conditions on your support. Don't tell her that if she doesn't do something about this problem, you won't be her friend anymore. This kind of threat will not work.

Offer empowering affirmations to help her see that she is a beautiful person and one that deserves love not abuse. Shelters have personal empowerment programs. There are self-esteem building classes. Your friend does not need to be a client of the shelter in order to receive help.

Listen to her and don't betray her trust. When she comes to you, she trusts you. You are there to help her, not the marriage.

Help her understand that she doesn't have to accept his estimation of her. She must trust her inner voice.

"What Else Can I Do?"

Give her a copy of this book. We designed it on purpose to be a quick read. The purpose is identification and inspiration. If your friend identifies as a victim, there is help in the book. The goal of the book is to help people understand this subtle and confusing type of abuse and to realize that it may be time to face the fear, see the signs, uncover the abuse, and discard the abuser — safely and secretly with a plan.

Resources:
More Communication
and The Joyful Heart

Mariska Hargitay, otherwise known as Olivia in the television show "Law and Order SVU," founded The Joyful Heart ten years ago. On her website, Mariska reveals that fan letters she received weren't about getting an autographed picture of her but they were women revealing, often for the first time, their stories of abuse. They moved her to begin her foundation. The foundation has raised over $15 million and served 14,000 people through its healing and wellness programs. The interesting and impressive story of her foundation is available on the website. **www.joyfulheartfoundation.org**

The foundation gained momentum when it recently joined with the NO MORE campaign, a very hopeful endeavor to end domestic violence and sexual assault. The NO MORE campaign is dedicated to:

- No more fear of the issues
- No more ignorance about the issues

- No more leaving it to others to find answers
- No more blaming survivors
- No more silence
- No more standing by and doing nothing

The No More campaign believes that increased conversation is the key to change. *"In NO MORE Study, two-thirds of Americans say that if we talk more about domestic violence and sexual assault, it would make it easier for them to help the victims."*

Hargitay produced a set of celebrity spots entitled "Speechless." They were the unscripted byproduct of a fall 2014 campaign by celebrities and NFL members in reaction to domestic violence in the NFL. Among others, Chris Meloni, Ice T., Andre Brougher, Hillary Swank, Tim Gunn, Mary J. Blige and Debra Messing reacted emotionally to the previous campaign.

The SVU star added, "Most simply put, we want these spots to bring these issues out of the darkness and into the light."

The Joyful Heart is one of many organizations participating in telling the world about this dirty little secret. By talking about it and raising awareness through speaking, victims are helped to become strong and come out of the shadows.

You Can Reach the Authors for Help

Tanya Brown: *Finding Peace Amid the Chaos: My Escape From Depression and Suicide* — www.TanyaBrown.net

Carolyn Inmon: Public speaker, professional speech writer and speech coach, author:
www.CarolynInmonStopDomesticAbuse.com

Our colleagues are ready to help you:

Kim Somers Egelsee: Her book *Getting Your Life to a 10+* has as its purpose to help build self esteem www.kimlifecoach.com

Tracy Kemble The W.I.N. Foundation: www.winfoundationinternational.org

Patricia Wenskunas: Crime Survivors: www.crimesurvivors.com

Non-Profit Organizations

Alliance for HOPE International: www.allianceforhope.com

American Bar Association Commission on Domestic and Sexual Violence: www.americanbar.org/groups/domestic_violence.html

Amnesty International: www.asafeplacedvs.org

A Safe Place, Inc.: www.asafeplacedvs.org

Asian & Pacific Islander Institute on Domestic Violence: www.apiidv.org

Battered Women's Justice Project: www.bwjp.org

Break the Cycle: www.breakthecycle.org

Care: www.my.care.org

Child Welfare League of America: www.cwla.org

Crisis Hotline: 954-324-7669

Domestic Shelters.org: www.domesticshelters.org

Equality Now: www.equalitynow.org

Futures Without Violence:
www.futureswitoutviolence.org

Help Guide: www.helpguide.org

Human Options: www.humanoptions.org

INCITE! Women of Color Against Violence:
www.incite-national.org

Institute of Domestic Violence in the African American Community: www.dvinstitute.org

Jewish Women International:
www.jewishwomen.org

Live Your Dream (Soroptimist): info@liveyourdream.org

Maitri: www.maitri.org

Manavi: www.manavi.org

Mending the Sacred Hoop: www.mshoop.org

National Center on Domestic and Sexual Violence:
www.ncdsv.org

National Coalition Against Domestic Violence:
www.ncadv.org

National Latino Alliance for the Elimination of Domestic Violence (ALIANZA): www.dvalianza.org

National Network to End Domestic Violence:
www.nnedv.org/projects/housing.html

No More: www.nomore.org/about

No More Tears: www.nmtproject.org

The Northwest Network: www.nwnetwork.org

Peace Over Violence: www.peaceoverviolence.org

Safe Horizon: www.safehorizon.org/domesticviolence

V-Day: www.vday.org/home

V.I.N.E.: www.vinelink.com

Women's Law Project: www.womenslawproject.org

The National Center on Domestic Violence, Trauma & Mental Health lists many more organizations:
www.nationalcenterdvtraumamh.org/resources/national-domestic-violence-organizations

Computer Caution

Please be careful when researching and reading about domestic abuse on your computer. An angry partner can find out what sites you are on or have been to. Many websites have clear and firm warnings. The National Network to End Domestic Violence has a warning on their website. It is titled safety alert and suggests the woman might consider a safer computer. The Women's Law Project also warns women and tells them that computers leave a trail that can be monitored.

Annual Awareness Campaigns

October: National Domestic Violence Awareness Month

October: Take Back the Night

November 25: International Day for the Elimination of Violence Against Women

Legislation

Legislation creates policy. You can help by keeping abreast of new legislation and supporting helpful laws. As a citizen, you can write letters and encourage others to do so.

Changing attitudes leads to changing laws. Help change attitudes in those around you including elected officials. At the least, you can show elected officials that your ideas will result in votes. At the most, you can change their hearts and minds.

GLOBAL: The International Violence Against Women Act (I-VAWA): This act would coordinate and improve existing U.S. foreign assistance efforts to stop this global crisis. www.amnestyusa.org

UNITED STATES: Women, Peace, and Security Act. This act was reintroduced on January 21, 2015 by Senators Barbara Boxer, Jeanne Shaheen and Mark Kirk. It will ensure the inclusion of women in conflict prevention, resolution and peacebuilding processes. www.womenthrive.org/blog/women-peace-and-security-act-reintroduced

STATE: To find the laws in your state which deal with such topics as restraining orders, visit Woman's Law Organization at: www.womenslaw.org/laws_state_type. php?statelaw_name=State%20Law%20Overview&state_code=GE

Government Organizations

Department of Justice (DOJ): www.justice.gov/ovw/domestic-violence

An Invitation to Stay Connected

This book was designed to help readers begin to identify Characters and any patterns of abuse they may have not seen before in their own lives and then take action and choose Real Love.

We believe that choosing Real Love begins with practicing Self-Love and Self-Care, and we want to invite you to download our online Self-Care and Overcoming Fear Support Tools:

Self-Care Tips to Use During Domestic Violence Chaos

Go to www.TanyaBrown.net and enter your name and email address to receive this support tool and to stay connected with Tanya and her causes.

Overcoming Fear

Go to www.CarolynInmonStopDomesticAbuse.com and enter your name and email address to receive this support tool and to stay connected with Carolyn and her causes.

There are also future books in development for the Batterer, Elder Abuse, and Children who have been abused, and this is a way for you to be one of the first to have access to that material.

About the Authors

Tanya Brown

Website: www.TanyaBrown.net

Tanya Brown is no stranger to adversity or trauma. Faced with near-overwhelming life challenges, Tanya used obstacles in her path to ultimately improve the quality of her life. She takes her life experience to audiences nationwide as a compelling motivational speaker, and she brings that experience to bear on her coaching practice. Her story makes it clear that you can overcome any adversity with the willingness to ask for help.

Tanya's Story of Loss, Grief, Depression... and Victory

The death of her sister Nicole Brown Simpson, which was sensationalized in the 1994 media frenzy featuring Nicole's husband O. J. Simpson, unleashed a flood of issues for Tanya. Prior to Nicole's murder, Tanya had lost several other loved ones, and emotional trauma was setting in. She engaged in dysfunctional eating patterns, and she busied herself with academic work as diversions from the mounting depression. Finally, in 2004, she suffered a breakdown that actually saved her life.

She worked for three months to get back on her feet with tools for managing her emotional well-being. Today, she is a celebrity author, a voice against domestic violence, and a motivational speaker and life coach who helps others bounce back from adversity.

Tanya has told her story in *Finding Peace Amid the Chaos*, an interesting and inspiring book.

Carolyn Inmon

Website: www.CarolynInmonStopDomesticAbuse.com
Facebook:www.facebook.com/pages/Carolyn-Inmon-Stop-Domestic-Abuse

Carolyn Inmon has devoted her entire life to serving families. Whether in the classroom where she taught over 10,000 students or in the community where she has volunteered to help victims of abuse, she has been the ultimate helper.

One of those students was a former foster youth who Carolyn mentored and helped her gain admittance to UC Berkeley where she was very successful academically. Unfortunately, a few years after graduating Phi Beta Kappa, the young woman took her own life. This tragedy was devastating for Carolyn, but it served as a turning point in her life, for she realized that high scholastic achievement is not enough. She dedicated herself to understanding how deep abuse and trauma affects people, helps determine their path in life, and rarely heals itself without help.

Upon retirement, Carolyn finally had time to give more fully to community service, with the prevention of abuse being the major topic. She took to the topic like a sponge – reading, researching, interviewing victims, writing, and speaking.

Because of her expertise in communication, Carolyn was quickly drawn to the abuse caused by words that hurt and damage the soul. She is known to ask the question, "Does it feel that your soul is sad?"

Carolyn has touched the lives of students she taught, the lives of the audience members who have heard her speak, and the lives of people who have read her words.

"I just wanted to make a difference," she once said. And, she is doing just that.